SELF-CARE JOURNAL FOR WOMEN

Self-Care Journal for Women

Prompts and Practices to Reflect and Embrace Your Best Life

MEGAN MacCUTCHEON, LPC, PMH-C

Wishing you joy on your self-care journey! ♥ Meg

ROCKRIDGE
PRESS

Interior and Cover Designer: Diana Haas, Amanda Kirk
Art Producer: Sue Bischofberger
Editor: Chloe Moffett
Production Editor: Holland Baker
Production Manager: Riley Hoffman

Illustration used under license from shutterstock.com
Author photo courtesy of Jamie Sutera Photography

Paperback ISBN: 978-1-63878-119-6
R0

THIS JOURNAL BELONGS TO:

____

"Because true belonging only happens when we present our authentic, imperfect selves to the world, our sense of belonging can never be greater than our level of self-acceptance."

—BRENÉ BROWN, *THE GIFTS OF IMPERFECTION*

CONTENTS

INTRODUCTION

Welcome to your very own self-care journal—a place where you can reflect upon the various aspects that contribute to living your best life. Whether you are facing a difficult time, feeling overwhelmed, or just crave a little more self-care in your routine, this journal will guide you through a variety of prompts and practices to help you be at your best.

My name is Megan, and I'm an author and therapist committed to helping people feel better and live their best lives. I especially love helping women build self-esteem and find tangible ways to improve their overall quality of life. I've learned so many tools, both personally and professionally, for improving self-care, and I'm excited to share many of them with you.

Self-care is an essential component to staying balanced and healthy in all areas of life—emotionally, physically, mentally, socially, professionally, and spiritually. But it's often overlooked or put on the back burner when life gets busy. The problem is that it's especially during times when you feel overwhelmed, burnt out, and exhausted that self-care is most vital.

Women tend to be nurturers and caretakers, but self-compassion and self-nurturing often take a back seat to everything else going on in life. It takes guidance and encouragement to learn how to put yourself first, treat yourself with kindness, and invest in your own well-being. This journal will help you do just that. You will have the opportunity to take a deep dive into exploring who you are and what you need in order to feel your best.

Self-care is all about nurturing yourself so that you can live a healthy, fulfilling, and abundant life. It involves active awareness of, and attempts to maintain, your well-being. But self-care doesn't have to be indulgent or overly time-consuming. Often, the best self-care just requires a little shift in how you think and how you treat yourself. It's about becoming clear on what you need, setting boundaries with others, and believing your needs are important, too.

While this journal is for all women, each woman's journey is unique. If certain affirmations don't fit, feel free to tailor them in ways that feel right for you so you can incorporate these encouraging statements into your daily thinking in your own way. It can help to write affirmations down in places you will see them often, as loving reminders to practice affirming your intrinsic value.

As you work through each section, show patience and kindness toward yourself. There is no wrong way to respond to prompts. As long as you take time to reflect and make room for self-care in your life, you are setting yourself on a path to wellness. It may take some time to find your rhythm and truly connect to yourself, but that's okay. Take your time, and know you deserve to feel supported, encouraged, respected, nourished, and fulfilled.

I am cheering you on, and it is my sincere hope that this journal will enhance your journey toward creating more balance and fulfillment in your life.

HOW TO USE THIS JOURNAL

Journaling allows us to access a different part of our brains than thinking or talking, in order to process emotions and untangle complicated feelings. I encourage you to use this book to reflect deeply, be vulnerable, and take an honest look at each aspect of your well-being. Imagine these pages as an extension of a community of women with similar self-care concerns and many of the same self-improvement goals. The more you get in touch with who you really are and open yourself up to new paths to wellness, the quicker you will understand what you truly need to feel your best.

This journal is divided into seven parts that correspond to core components of self-care. By exploring the prompts and trying out various practical exercises, you'll be able to establish your own self-care practice. Each prompt will elicit self-reflection and give you space to connect to yourself. Motivating quotes and affirmations are offered to help inspire you on your journey. Through the practices, you can try out new strategies and tools to help you establish and maintain a routine of self-care and a more fulfilling relationship with yourself, others, and the world around you. Feel free to move through this journal at your own pace, spending extra time with areas to which you feel most drawn or in which you need the most help.

Each thoughtful prompt includes dedicated space to write. Reflect in whatever way is most helpful to you, be that stream of consciousness, bulleted lists, sketches, or just jotted-down words and ideas. The aim is to get you into a comfortable routine of meaningful journaling to aid in self-exploration and the development of healthy self-care practices. If you need more space, please feel free to grab an additional notebook and let it all flow.

Sometimes the process of journaling and reflecting inward can feel like going through a tunnel—the darkest part is in the middle. At times, you may feel overwhelmed by emotions. I encourage you to keep going, knowing there's always a light at the end of the tunnel. If, however, at any point you feel flooded with feelings of depression, anxiety, grief, or anger that feel unbearable, please reach out to a qualified mental health provider to help you unravel and work through complicated emotions.

This journal is not a replacement for treatment or therapy, but rather one tool that can help you along the way. It's a great way to work through complex feelings and explore new concepts. Self-care involves seeking additional help when necessary, and you deserve to surround yourself with a support system that will help you live a satisfying and rewarding life.

"Life is like an onion: You peel it off one layer at a time, and sometimes you weep."

—CARL SANDBURG

PART 1

Emotional Self-Care

Emotional stability and the ability to stay grounded amid the ups and downs of life are key to every person's overall well-being. Ironically, it's one area that we usually don't learn a lot about until we're already struggling emotionally in one way or another. Emotional self-care involves learning to acknowledge the inevitable emotions we all face as humans and open ourselves to embracing effective ways to cope with them. As you explore your own relationship to your various feelings and beliefs about expressing them, consider what mindful shifts might allow you to take better care of your emotional self.

I recognize my capacity to feel numerous emotions and allow myself to feel my feelings.

Feelings are part of the human experience; however, sometimes we receive messages that certain emotions are bad or wrong. We may cut ourselves off from powerful emotions or bottle them up and avoid them.

Consider the following emotions and reflect upon your experience with each. Are there feelings you try to reject or hide? Where does your reaction come from? How might things shift when you give yourself permission to experience your feelings?

shame › anxiety › sadness › depression › disappointment › grief › fear › despair › scorn › hate › acceptance › optimism › hope › empathy › love › trust › joy

My feelings are not optional; however, what I do with them is within my control.

When we try to suppress emotions, we risk them eventually erupting. We don't have a choice in what feelings bubble up during certain experiences or encounters; however, we *do* have a choice in how we handle those emotions. Think about your strong emotions. Do you accept them as they come and contemplate the best approach for coping in the moment? Do you try to sweep the feelings under the rug? Or do you lash out? Reflect on your typical responses and consider what shifts you could make to handle emotions more effectively.

I acknowledge my emotions and allow myself to move through them.

Bottling up emotions is counterproductive to self-care. We don't have to welcome painful or difficult emotions, but it helps to accept their presence. It can be as simple as stating to yourself, *I am feeling intense anger.* This acknowledgment alone can lessen some of the pressure. From there, you can allow yourself to move through the emotion toward relief. Jot down the various emotions you experience over the next few weeks and practice acknowledging what you are feeling. Contemplate what you might do to honor each feeling before releasing it.

I find healthy outlets and embrace new ways to cope with my emotions.

There are lots of ways to cope with difficult emotions. Some coping methods are aligned with self-care, and others are destructive and self-sabotaging. If you've engaged in the latter in any form (such as running from emotions, engaging in self-harm, or acting aggressively), don't beat yourself up. You were likely coping the best you could at the time. But there are healthier options. Write about a few times you dealt with an emotion in a damaging way. What would you like to do differently the next time a similar emotion arises?

I acknowledge that everyone feels, expresses, and copes with emotions differently.

While all humans experience the same range of emotions, two people facing the exact same situation might react in two completely different ways. There's no one correct way to handle emotions, but differences in coping styles can lead to conflict and distance in relationships. Consider whether you've had conflict in your relationships because of differences in handling emotions. Are there ways you can better empathize with, or react to, the ways others cope? How can a better understanding of your own way of coping and a commitment to communicating your needs help you in the future?

I recognize that there is no right or wrong when it comes to experiencing various emotions.

There's no way to predict how long it will take to move through challenging emotions. Grief, for example, is both a feeling and a process that involves many other emotions—anger, sadness, disbelief, despair, desperation—often cycled through in no particular order. Recall times in your life when you've experienced intense emotions. Did you spend time worrying about how you *should* be feeling? What might have been different if you could accept where you were and put your energy into finding ways to keep moving through it?

I grant myself the same level of respect, compassion, and permission to feel as I would give a loved one.

Why is it that we have so much more compassion, tolerance, patience, and empathy for friends and loved ones going through a rough time than we do for ourselves? When you're feeling overwhelmed by emotions, stop and consider how you would respond to a friend in the same spot, then treat yourself with the same level of compassion. Write about the differences in how you treat yourself versus how you treat others. Consider what you could do to be a better friend to yourself, especially during challenging times.

I welcome support and ask for help when needed.

Are you great at offering help but not so good at asking for it? When we don't ask for and accept help, we run the risk of letting frustration, resentment, and exhaustion build up to the point of burnout. Consider areas in which you wish you had more support. Think about who does or doesn't offer help and why. Sometimes we need to recognize that others are not mind readers but might be willing to step up and pitch in if we just ask. What could you do to request and accept more help in your life?

I forgive myself for mistakes and recognize that mistakes are how we learn and grow.

We all make mistakes, and an important part of self-care involves learning to forgive ourselves. Rather than getting caught up in self-blame and shame, try to become open to seeing the opportunities for growth, no matter how big these mistakes might be. What mistakes have you made? What learning opportunities can you take away? Think about some things you've felt guilty or shameful about. Focus on how these experiences can help you grow. Write yourself a gentle letter of forgiveness.

Close your eyes and visualize a container with a lid. Imagine all of your worries, stressors, tension, fears, and painful emotions going into this container—picture them as liquid, objects, words on paper, or whatever you want. Take your time putting every last negative or stressful thing into this container. When you're done, imagine putting the lid on the container, sealing it up, and placing it somewhere out of sight, but where you can access it later. Imagine yourself walking away, closing any drawers or doors. Notice what it feels like to get some space from the things that weigh you down, knowing you can go back and deal with them once you have a little more energy to cope. Practice this exercise regularly.

"But self-kindness involves more than merely stopping self-judgment. It involves actively comforting ourselves, responding just as we would to a dear friend in need. It means we allow ourselves to be emotionally moved by our own pain, stopping to say, 'This is really difficult right now.'"

—KRISTIN NEFF, *SELF-COMPASSION*

"The most terrifying thing is to accept oneself completely."

—CARL JUNG

PART 2

Physical Self-Care

Physical self-care involves a concerted effort to take care of our health and appreciate our body for all it does. Often, when women think about their physical selves, they groan, fixating on their flaws and feeling inadequate. This section will help you focus on appreciating your physical well-being. Regardless of where you are with healthy habits or thoughts surrounding body image, you can begin to recognize how powerful your body really is. As you practice affirming and developing gratitude for your physical well-being, you'll naturally be inspired to put forth effort to maintain physical health so that you can feel your best from the inside out.

I appreciate my body for all it can do.

So many women struggle with body image, thanks to unhelpful messages and unrealistic societal ideals regarding how we "should" look. Today, focus on how great your body really is. Think of all the things your body can do—breathe, pump blood, think, feel. If you can move, hug, or eat a delicious meal, then you have a lot to be grateful for. The body is truly amazing. List all the functions you appreciate your body doing, and take a moment to thank it for all it does to support you.

I accept the uniqueness of my body and my appearance.

As women, we often spend a lot of time and energy focusing on what we perceive as flaws. Pause to recognize how unique we all really are. Think about all the different traits, shapes, sizes, colors, textures, and differences among women. There is only one you, and you have your own unique qualities to celebrate. Today, take a step back, silence your inner critic for a moment, and write about the things you *do* appreciate about your appearance and unique traits.

I choose foods that nourish my body and bring me strength.

We don't have much choice when it comes to the body type and physical traits we're born with, but we do have great control of how we take care of our body and the food choices we make. Take some time to consider your diet and eating habits. Which aspects do you feel good about? Which habits would you like to change and why? What conscious decisions can you make to ensure you are nourishing and respecting your body?

I embrace moderation when it comes to caring for my physical well-being.

Dedication to a mission can cause us to operate in extremes. Perhaps we want to run three miles every day or entirely cut out sugar and desserts. Extremes like these often backfire. Rather than setting lofty, rigid goals, we can embrace moderation when it comes to diet and exercise habits and allow for inevitable setbacks. This might look like running a mile *a few times* a week or enjoying an occasional dessert. What goals would you like to set to enhance your physical health, and how can you ensure they are flexible?

My body is powerful and made to sweat.

Exercise improves both physical and mental health. It's important to know and accept your limits, but don't be afraid to trust in your body's strength as you engage in exercise and physical activities you enjoy. What type of workouts do you enjoy, and how often are you incorporating exercise into your weekly routine? Do you experience any limitations to physical activity; if so, how can you safely work around them? Are there any types of exercise you'd like to try? Write down a commitment to try something new this month.

I allow my body to move and use movement to maintain balance.

Movement is essential for keeping the mind, body, and spirit in balance. Many of us wind up being fairly stagnant throughout our days, especially if we work in an office environment. Consider your typical day. How often do you move around? Write about what kinds of movement are easy for you and feel good for your body. Perhaps you can take a moment every hour to stretch your arms and upper body. Maybe you could walk around the block after dinner. What can you commit to doing to incorporate more movement into your day?

I set physical boundaries that protect my own space and well-being and stand up to those who disrespect my limits.

Part of caring for ourselves involves being aware of our limits—and enforcing them—in protecting our physical space and body. We are in charge of our own body and have the right to determine who can touch us and when. Consider if there are any aspects of your life in which you don't feel physically safe or comfortable. Why does this happen? What steps can you take to better protect yourself going forward?

I allow myself quality rest in order to heal and replenish my energy.

Rest and sleep are vital to health. Sleep allows our body time to grow, heal, and rejuvenate. Write about your sleep habits. Do you give yourself time to unwind at the end of the day? Do you have a consistent routine before bed? Are you able to get quality sleep every night? How do you feel after a good night's rest versus a poor one? If you struggle with getting to bed or falling or staying asleep, what could you do to improve your sleep habits?

I make time to maintain my physical well-being.

It's easy to get so wrapped up in the busyness of life that we ignore self-care tasks like scheduling annual doctor and dentist appointments. If you tend to push off the things that maintain and monitor your well-being, this is a sign that it's time to prioritize yourself. Make a list of everything you need to stay current with your health maintenance. Are there things you've been putting off? If so, why do you think that is? What would make it easier to take the time to care for yourself?

In this calming exercise, you'll use the four elements—earth, water, fire, and air—to mindfully check in and focus attention on your physical being.

Earth: Press your feet into the floor or your hands or other body part into a table or firm surface. Feel the surface beneath you. This is a wonderful way to reconnect to your physical body and feel grounded in the present.

Water: Drink a glass of water. It's so important to stay hydrated. Drinking water activates your digestive system and helps your internal organs function.

Fire: Ignite your imagination and think of something you can do today to feel physically balanced.

Air: Take a few deep, slow, cleansing breaths in and out. Inhale tranquility, and exhale any stress or tension.

“Loving everything about yourself—even the unacceptable—is an act of personal power. It is the beginning of healing.”

—CHRISTIANE NORTHRUP, MD

"Forces beyond your control can take away everything you possess except one thing, your freedom to choose how you will respond to the situation."

—VIKTOR FRANKL, ***MAN'S SEARCH FOR MEANING***

PART 3

Psychological Self-Care

Psychological self-care is a key component to feeling your best and navigating the ups and downs of life with strength, resilience, and positivity. Our thought processes impact our mental well-being, and a healthy inner dialogue helps us stay balanced and push through challenges. This section will help you pay attention to your self-talk, to ensure that the messages you internalize are encouraging and empowering, rather than self-berating and critical. Sometimes it feels easier said than done, but we do have a choice in the attitude we take in any given situation. Choosing positivity and self-compassion is the difference-maker in navigating life successfully.

I maintain self-compassion and make my well-being a priority.

Think about the expectations you put on yourself and the way you react when you make mistakes. Do you beat yourself up? Or do you demonstrate the same level of self-compassion that you would offer a loved one? It's easy to fall into a habit of relentless self-judgment and criticism, but this only undermines your well-being. Write about a few times you were hard on yourself and what you could have said or thought instead. What can you say to yourself the next time you make a mistake to remind yourself to be understanding?

I identify unhelpful thought patterns and reframe them into messages that better serve me.

Humans are wired to focus on negatives—we commonly engage in self-sabotaging habits of harsh, critical, and self-deprecating thinking. It takes effort and active awareness to notice when our thinking is setting us up to feel anxious, depressed, or overly self-critical. Common patterns of distorted thinking include all-or-nothing thinking, minimizing achievements, magnifying mistakes, labeling yourself with mean names, and personalizing everything. Pay attention to your inner dialogue and jot down any thoughts that include negative or distorted self-talk. Can you reframe these critical messages into sentences that are more kind and encouraging?

I can choose my attitude and decide to embrace the silver linings even when things are difficult or distressing.

Challenging circumstances and setbacks are inevitable in life. We cannot choose to avoid pain, and the feelings that painful situations evoke are not optional. We can, however, choose the attitude we will take in response. Think about challenging situations in your life. How have you dealt with them previously? Did those methods help you feel at peace? How might a shift in perspective or attitude help you navigate challenging times with more grace, optimism, and perseverance?

I understand that words are powerful. I choose words wisely and avoid language that holds me back or puts me down.

When we think in rigid ways, using words like *should*, *must*, *have to*, or *need to*, we set ourselves up for frustration and feelings of failure. These words don't allow any flexibility or room for error. While it may seem simplistic, subtle shifts in language can make a big difference in how you feel. Write about times you tell yourself *I should*, *I must*, or *I have to*. How might you experience less pressure or disappointment if you were to instead tell yourself, *I would like to* or *I choose to*?

I recognize situations, relationships, and dynamics that are unhealthy for me and choose to create distance to preserve my well-being.

Difficult relationships and interpersonal drama can take a huge toll on our mental well-being. Part of practicing self-care involves actively monitoring the relationships in our life and recognizing when certain situations are dragging us down. Make a list of the people in your life with whom you interact regularly—family, friends, coworkers, neighbors. Which of these relationships feel mutually supportive and nurturing? Which feel burdensome or damaging? If you identify relationships that feel detrimental to your well-being, what can you do to create distance or set stronger boundaries to protect yourself?

I recognize my limitations, refrain from placing impossible demands on myself, and allow others to support me.

Sometimes we get the message that women should be superhuman, capable of juggling everything with ease, but the reality is, this isn't always possible. Sometimes we need to say no, delegate to others, and accept that we require help. If it's hard for you to lower your personal standards and accept limitations regarding how much you can take on, consider what gets in the way. Pride? People pleasing? Fear of being seen as incompetent, weak, or uncaring? How can you relieve the pressure you put on yourself?

I make time for rest and relaxation.

Making time to relax and unwind is vital to staying balanced and keeping our overall well-being in check, but sometimes women are so busy managing everything and taking care of others that we fail to take time for ourselves. Think about how often you take time to relax. Do you need to make adjustments in your life to allow for more downtime? What are your favorite ways to unwind and recharge? Make a plan to do several of these activities regularly over the next month.

I set goals that are realistic and achievable.

Many people set unrealistic goals and wind up feeling defeated. It's important to leave some room for the unavoidable setbacks or curveballs that life may throw your way. When you set small goals that you can build upon, you're more likely to succeed and stay motivated. Think about some goals you've set for yourself. Are they realistic and achievable? List a few complex or difficult goals that you may have struggled to reach. How could you break these bigger goals down into smaller steps?

I seek assistance when I need help processing life's challenges and dealing with overwhelming emotions.

Challenging situations and relationships can be overwhelming. It's unrealistic to assume you should be able to handle it all yourself. If you're struggling in some area of your life, getting into therapy can help you process your experience and learn new ways to cope. Seeking support shows strength, but that's not always the message we receive. Consider where in your life you're struggling. Do certain thoughts, beliefs, or fears of judgment hold you back from getting help? What could you do to allow yourself the gift of being supported?

Start paying close attention to the various thoughts going through your mind all day long. We all have a stream of inner dialogue, but typically we're not aware of what those thoughts are. Sometimes all we notice is the feeling the thought evokes. Start with your feelings. When you are feeling an emotion, stop and consider where it's coming from. Dig deep into your mind and consider what thoughts might be causing the emotion. If you put your thoughts into sentence form, what would they say? Assess the level of self-compassion in your self-talk. Then work to reframe any harsh or critical language into kinder words. By practicing this exercise regularly, you'll literally rewire your brain to improve self-care.

"It's only a thought and a thought can be changed. I am not limited by any past thinking. I choose my thoughts with care."

—LOUISE HAY

"Treat yourself the way you would a cherished friend. You forgive her faults. You tolerate her flaws and mistakes. You cut her lots of slack and you accept her just the way she is, not how you would like her to be."

—STEPHANIE MARSTON

PART 4

Social Self-Care

Humans are social creatures—we are biologically wired to connect to one another. Research demonstrates multiple health benefits of social support, but interpersonal interactions are complex and can lead to all types of dynamics—some that build us up, and others that drag us down. When we aren't feeling our best, we might isolate ourselves or stay stuck in unhealthy relationships. Social self-care involves believing that you're deserving of connections that support you. Start by becoming your own supportive best friend, then work to surround yourself with a network of people who enrich your life and help you feel and be your best.

I form connections that are nurturing and bring me joy, laughter, and a sense of community.

Nurturing, loving, and supportive connections are essential to a sense of belonging that keeps us grounded and fulfilled. Think about your network of family and friends. Who are the people who bring you joy? Who can you turn to for support, helpful advice, or a shoulder to lean on? Think about how much time you spend with these people. If your supportive connections are lacking, how can you commit to forming new friendships or get involved with others to build your own village and feel more connected?

I distance myself from harmful people and toxic relationships.

Think again about the people in your life and consider whether any of your relationships bring you down, keep you stuck in unhealthy dynamics, or make you question your worth. How can you create distance from these people? Perhaps there are family members or colleagues you cannot completely avoid, but you can work at blocking their negativity from impacting you by shifting how you think about or react to their words or actions. What measures can you take to better protect yourself?

I establish healthy limits and enforce them assertively with others.

Consider how you react when people disrespect you or cross your boundaries. Do you tend to act passively? Aggressively? Self-care includes assertively enforcing boundaries and effectively responding in instances when you feel disrespected. Assertiveness is about clearly stating your wants and needs, but in a manner that is also respectful of the other person. Think about situations in which you experienced conflict, and consider how you reacted. What could you have done to act more assertively? What changes would you like to make regarding how you deal with conflict and confrontation?

I avoid comparing myself unfavorably to others and instead respect my own unique journey.

It's really easy in our society—especially with social media—to feel badly about ourselves in comparison to what we see or believe to be true about others. Think about the images, advertisements, or messages that make you feel "less than" or not good enough. What comparisons do you make between yourself and others? What steps could you take to distance yourself from the things that bring you down, and what shifts could you make in your self-talk to refrain from comparisons?

I respect who I am and enjoy sharing my unique traits with those who appreciate me.

Presidential adviser Bernard Baruch stated, "Be who you are and say what you feel because those who mind don't matter and those who matter don't mind." You're inevitably going to encounter people who, for whatever reason, may not like you. Maybe you have different likes and interests, or different senses of humor, or maybe you simply remind them of somebody else. How much do you worry about what others think? Why do their opinions matter? Write about steps you can take that focus on liking yourself rather than worrying about the opinions of others.

I do not allow criticism, judgment, or unkindness from others to define who I am.

We are all constant works in progress, and there is no such thing as perfection. When you're faced with criticism or judgment, stop and consider whether it is valid. If so, focus on what changes you would like to make. If unfounded, choose to let it go and move forward. Think about times when you've been criticized or unfavorably judged by others. How did you react? How would you like to react in the future? What mindset can help you do this?

I know my own needs and wants in relationships, and give myself permission to pursue what brings me peace and happiness.

We are all unique. We have our own personality and individual needs and wants in life and relationships, and they are valid. Think about what your needs are and whether they are being met. For example, are you introverted or extroverted? Do you need some space or alone time to recharge your battery? Do you crave togetherness and wish for more connection? What do you need more or less of in your relationships? Challenge yourself to increase your awareness of your own needs and wants. Consider how you can go after what you desire.

I have compassion for others and am open-minded about everyone's unique journeys.

We have a social responsibility to respect one another and demonstrate compassion. As the How Full Is Your Bucket? books demonstrate, when we "dip from someone else's bucket," we dip from our own as well. We don't have to agree with everyone's views or actions—it's about being respectful of differences and remaining assertive (rather than aggressive) in interactions. Think about the people in your life who push your buttons, and consider times of conflict with them. What shifts can help you keep the peace while also protecting yourself?

I am responsible for my own actions, not for other people's reactions.

Sometimes it's difficult to separate responsibility for our own actions from responsibility for the actions, reactions, and feelings of others. We are responsible for being kind and respectful, but we're not responsible for how others react to our decisions, opinions, requests, and boundaries. Do you spend a lot of time worrying about how your actions impact others? Are you a people pleaser? Consider how often you worry over things out of your control, and journal about ways you can release yourself from that burden.

Think about people who create problems in your life or who have hurt you or caused pain. Write a letter to each one, expressing your feelings and saying whatever you want to say. Don't hold back. Pour all your thoughts and emotions onto the page, then find a way to accept what happened—not to let the person off the hook, but to release yourself from carrying the burden any longer. When you are done, shred or burn the letter if you'd like. Or you may choose to give the letter (or an edited version of it) to the person. Whatever you choose, know that this exercise is meant to be a cathartic, healing experience just for you.

"Tend to your friendship garden, weeding and pruning the stuff that has stopped growing and focus on that which continues to flower and bring you joy."

—TORY JOHNSON, *SHIFT FOR GOOD*

"Success is a journey, not a destination."

—ARTHUR ASHE

PART 5

Professional Self-Care

Professional self-care isn't just about career—it's about considering the various roles that form your identity—daughter, sister, partner, mother, friend, employee, boss—and ensuring work-life balance. Whether your work earns a salary or involves being an unpaid caretaker to others, think about all the responsibilities that keep you busy. Do you feel fulfilled? Are you overwhelmed? In this section, "work" refers to any responsibilities you juggle, paid or not. The goals in addressing professional self-care are to ensure you have balance in your life and to give yourself permission to feel good about the work you do.

I make professional decisions with confidence, honoring what is in my best interest.

What does "professional identity" mean to you? Are you currently working at a paying job? In school? A caretaker? Balancing career and home life can be incredibly challenging for women. It's hard to "have it all," and sometimes difficult decisions need to be made to prioritize the different aspects. Whether you are earning a salary or not, you are working in some capacity. Consider what that looks like for you, and write about where you are now, where you've been, and where you hope to be in the future.

I believe in myself, embrace my potential for growth, and have confidence in my ability to contribute something good and worthwhile to the world.

Finding meaning and purpose in daily life is key to feeling fulfilled and motivated to keep moving forward. Think about how the things you do every day make a difference in your family, your company, your community, or the world. It's easy to get so bogged down by the minutiae of everyday tasks that you lose sight of the bigger picture. Stop and consider how you are contributing on a broader level. What about your various roles is important? How do you feel when you recognize these contributions?

I pursue work I enjoy and feel good about.

Consider how you feel about your work. What led you to whatever you are doing? Have you been able to follow your dreams, or did you feel pressure to fulfill someone else's wishes? Do you feel a sense of passion for your work, or do you feel stuck in a rut, going through the motions to earn a paycheck or keep things running without any real pleasure? What would it take to increase the joy you experience regarding your work? What steps can you take to move toward greater satisfaction?

I know what I need and want in my life/job/career path, and I am proactive about moving in a direction that fulfills my dreams.

It can be challenging to take steps to achieve an ideal work scenario. Doing so may involve stepping outside your comfort zone and doing things that feel scary. If, in the last prompt, you identified things that could make your work more enjoyable, what has held you back from pursuing them? What fears or obstacles have gotten in your way? How can you maintain clarity regarding what you truly want, and what steps would you need to take to make your vision a reality?

I recognize that some paths are merely stepping-stones to something greater.

Do you feel trapped in a role you don't love, or have you yet to discover a fulfilling job? Our attitudes can make a big difference in our overall happiness and ability to see the bigger picture. If you are stuck in work you don't enjoy, what could you do to accept the situation for the time being, as you look toward making changes? Are there any silver linings to what you are currently doing? Are you mastering any skill sets that might be useful in the future? What perspective can make things easier?

I prioritize self-care while juggling my responsibilities.

Many women experience the "second shift"—coming home from work to a host of other responsibilities for the family. Author Nora Roberts describes it as juggling various balls—some are glass and others are plastic, she explains. Knowing which is which is key. Think about how well you balance professional and home-life responsibilities. Which balls are glass? Which responsibilities are vital, and which can be forfeited on days you feel burnt out? What balls can you let go of to ensure that self-care remains a priority?

I trust my decisions and take action to support my long-term best interests.

Trusting our gut and acting in our best interest when it comes to professional goals and endeavors can feel challenging—it may even be risky at times. Things like leaving a job, requesting accommodations for a better work-life balance, or asking for a raise can be hard! Women in particular tend to struggle with advocating for themselves. What challenges have you faced in trying to improve your satisfaction level in the work you do? What steps could you take to feel more confident in improving any areas that are lacking?

I appreciate various outlooks and differences in opinions. I navigate conflict with an open mind and a commitment to mutual respect.

Regardless of the type of work you do, you are inevitably going to face conflict or potential personality clashes at one time or another. Whether disagreements arise with your business partner, client, employee, or teenager, it can be hard to keep cool and navigate the situation from a place of composure. Think about conflicts you've had in the past. Do you feel proud of the way you handled them, or is there something you wish you'd done differently? What commitments would you like to make to yourself around handling future conflict?

I am open to learning, expanding my knowledge, and embracing new opportunities that help me grow.

Life is constantly changing, and even things we don't consider learning opportunities can teach us valuable lessons or equip us with new skills and knowledge. Think about any recent struggles or even the most mundane experiences, and consider how they might provide tools that could benefit you or help you grow. What takeaways could be useful in the future? If you feel stagnant in any area of your life, what could you do to ignite a sense of excitement, wonder, or possibility?

On a large sheet of paper, make a time line of your life, from birth to the present. Jot down every role, position, job, or growth opportunity you've experienced. Next, think about how each experience has shaped you into the person you are today. What experiences are you grateful for? Which were the most challenging? Which opportunities helped move you forward? Are there any experiences or roles that held you back or made you feel stuck? Think about where you would like to be in the future. What's your ideal scenario? What would make you feel most fulfilled? Spend some time journaling as if those things have already happened.

"It's never too late to be what you might have been."

—GEORGE ELIOT

"Clutter is not just the stuff on your floor. It's anything that stands between you and the life you want to be living."

—PETER WALSH

PART 6

Environmental Self-Care

Environmental self-care involves noticing the world around you and considering the environments in which you spend the most time—your home, your office, your car, and your community. The character and conditions of your surroundings directly correlate to your mental well-being. How you dress, what you own, and how you take care of your surroundings convey messages—both subconsciously and consciously—to yourself and others around you. Spend some time exploring your various environments, and consider how tweaking the places and spaces you occupy with a mind toward comfort, good feelings, and pride of ownership can be a form of self-care to ultimately improve your overall well-being.

I'm creating an environment that fosters my well-being.

Tidying expert Marie Kondo made famous the concept of surveying each object in your home to determine whether or not it sparks joy. Let's wrap our brain around the idea that the things in our environment impact us emotionally. Take a moment to get in touch with how you are affected by various items in your home. Identify at least 5 to 10 objects around you, and write about how they make you feel. Is there something that makes you happy? Anything you don't like? What colors, shapes, or textures impact you and in what ways?

I create joy and contentment in my surroundings.

Quantum physics and energy science describe how humans and "stuff" are all made of energy. Everything is constantly interacting, energetically affecting one another in various ways. Survey your surroundings and determine whether your environment is an energetic match for things you want—such as happiness, wellness, and all the good you strive for in your life. If you've identified things you don't like, how can you manipulate objects in your environment to make shifts or changes? How can you create a space free from things that bring you down?

My home embraces and protects me.

"Your home should rise up to greet you," says designer Nate Berkus. Imagine yourself walking through your front door. If your home could talk, what would it say to greet you? Do you feel happy and safe walking into your home? Or do you feel something negative? Repeat this exercise with each area of your home. Try it with your car, office, or any surroundings that you frequent. What changes can you make that will ensure each space feels safe and nurturing?

I easily let go of the things that no longer serve me.

As you thought about various spaces in your life, did you identify any areas of clutter? Clutter can both reflect and contribute to mental chaos. It can be hard to let go of certain items, but remember that memories are in the mind, not in that old, unworn concert T-shirt or stack of papers collecting dust. How does the idea of getting rid of some belongings make you feel? How can you set realistic and manageable goals toward eliminating clutter? Start by making lists. What items could you consider throwing away? What can you donate?

I take charge of my surroundings to keep me feeling balanced and whole.

Organization comes naturally to some people, but you don't have to be Martha Stewart to embrace the connection between self-care and maintaining your environment. What does organization mean to you? Are there items that you'd like to have more easily accessible? What methods of organizing and end results would make you feel supported and nurtured in your space? Once you've identified goals, look for tips, tools, and systems to help you activate a plan. Google away and jot down ideas you'd like to implement.

I make decisions that support me in feeling my best.

Small everyday decisions, such as what clothes you put on, what types of food you eat, and which items you purchase for your home and lifestyle, influence how you feel. Take note of decisions you feel good about—ones that help you feel happy, healthy, and whole. Consider decisions you regret, or ones that contribute to guilt or insecurity. How can you bring more clarity and intention into the everyday decisions you make, in order to feel your best? What are some philosophies you can embrace?

I respect nature and appreciate its ability to replenish my energy.

Step outdoors, either physically or as a visualization. Get some distance from material objects and electronics. Do you have a grassy area or garden just steps outside your home? Or do you have to go far to find a place of stillness? How does being outside in nature make you feel? What spaces or landscapes make you feel most at peace? How often are you able to enjoy your favorite spots outdoors? Would you benefit from spending more time appreciating the world around you? If so, what plans can you make to get outside more often?

I feel connected to my community and embrace all it has to offer.

We all have interesting places in our communities, but many of us don't take advantage of them often enough. Are there places near you that you've never even visited? Maybe you only take advantage of sightseeing when visitors come to town. What are the places in your community that you vibe with? What places make you feel happy and alive? How can you make a commitment to visit them more often? To get started, think of parks, coffee shops, museums, concert venues, restaurants, local shops, historic sites, and places in nature.

I take care of the world around me, and it takes care of me.

There's so much the world has to offer: breathtaking scenery, foods that sustain us, and resources that support our lives are just a few. Consider how you relate to the world. Do you stop to appreciate beautiful landscapes and sunsets? Do you consciously care for the world by making clean lifestyle choices? Think about how often you pause to notice all that the world has to offer. Do you tend to take things for granted? What steps could you take to better appreciate the world around you?

Close your eyes and imagine a perfect place. Take your time, and experience it through each of your five senses. Then open your eyes and notice how your imaginary place compares to your current surroundings. What three elements can you identify in your imaginary place that you can make a point to bring into your home and life? Perhaps a live plant or fresh flowers. Maybe an essential oil diffuser with a pleasant scent. Are there textures you enjoy—a soft blanket on your couch? Is there a flavor of tea you love? While we can't always create a perfect utopia, we can become mindful of the power of bringing elements into our surroundings that create joy and provide self-nurturing.

"The space in which we live should be for the person we are becoming now, not for the person we were in the past."

—MARIE KONDO

"People are like stained-glass windows. They sparkle and shine when the sun is out, but when the darkness sets in, their true beauty is revealed only if there is a light from within."

—ELISABETH KÜBLER-ROSS

PART 7

Spiritual Self-Care

Spiritual self-care involves exploring your beliefs surrounding your connection to the world, and developing rituals and practices that help you feel grounded despite not having definitive answers to some of the mysteries of life. Your sense of spirituality allows you to connect deeply to your highest self—the self that is the "real you," separate from your ego, fears, and struggles. For many people, spirituality overlaps with religious beliefs and practices, but it's not necessary to have any type of religious foundation to explore and practice spiritual self-care. Just consider your spirit as your true self.

I explore my sense of connectedness to the world around me.

Nobody knows for sure answers to questions like *What is the meaning of life?* or *Is there a God?* What has your experience been with making sense of these existential questions and defining spirituality for yourself? Regardless of your specific beliefs, you are here, living this life, reading this book, and working on self-improvement. How do you make sense of your life and purpose? How do you feel about your life and sense of connectedness to the world on the whole? What are your thoughts about your spiritual self?

I am in control of my spiritual belief system and define my beliefs in a way that feels right for me.

Think about the religious or spiritual teachings you have been exposed to throughout your life. What beliefs and practices resonate with you today and support you in your self-care journey? Are there traditions or rituals that you would like to adopt or continue to embrace? Do you struggle with feeling like you *should* maintain certain beliefs, even if they don't feel right for you? What would it take to feel confident in your own choices and relationship to your spiritual well-being?

I distance myself from concepts that I disagree with or that obstruct taking care of my true self.

We have the right to choose for ourselves the beliefs and practices that support us in feeling grounded, whole, and securely connected to the world around us. Did you grow up with any teachings that were imposed on you that don't feel right to your journey now? How can you separate yourself from ideas or practices that no longer resonate with you? What can you do to feel comfortable releasing beliefs or practices that feel harmful or disconnected from who you want to be?

I open my mind to new ideas and embrace what resonates with me.

Part of self-care involves continuously learning, being open to new ideas, and making conscious decisions about what works for you in supporting your highest self. Are there any belief systems or traditions that you are curious about? Are you open to new ideas? If not, what stands in your way? Maybe you feel comfortable in your current beliefs. Or maybe you think you need permission from others. Perhaps you want to learn more first. How can you allow yourself to be open to and seek out new ideas that further your spiritual growth?

I choose to believe that my life has meaning, even if that meaning is not yet clear to me.

Think about what your purpose or meaning may be. Do you have a sense of the difference you make in the world and to those around you, or do you struggle to find reason and meaning in what you do? Are you willing to believe that your life has some purpose or meaning, even if you aren't yet clear on how you fit into the bigger scheme of things? What action steps could you take to help you find meaning and affirm your worth? Are there passions you could pursue in the interest of finding a greater sense of purpose?

I maintain rituals and practices that help me feel grounded and whole.

Think about the various rituals and practices in your life. What helps you feel grounded and present? Are there important practices or routines in your day or week? What types of traditions are important for you around holidays or important dates? If you've been remiss in upholding the practices you enjoy or haven't made time to embrace the things you truly love, how can you make a commitment to yourself to prioritize these things? What are three practices you can do more regularly to nourish your spirit?

I make time for moments of stillness.

Many of us live in a busy world filled with a lot of noise. Stress, responsibilities, technology, instant access, news, and social media all compete with our ability to tune in to our inner wisdom and feel a sense of calm. Connecting to our spiritual essence requires us to occasionally pause and focus inward. How often are you able to escape your stressors and find moments of stillness? How can you make a commitment to increase moments of silence and tranquility to connect more deeply to your highest self?

I am introspective and self-reflective, striving to grow and become the best possible version of myself.

What do you notice when you stop and look inward? When you grant yourself time to be silent, are you able to gain some perspective to better understand your feelings, needs, and wants? Stopping to reflect can help you recognize things in your life that aren't working well and give you moments of clarity to determine what changes to make moving forward. What's working? What's not? What shifts can you make in your life in order to feel and be your best?

I honor my own spirit and take pride in who I am.

As we come to the last prompt on your self-care journey, stop and reflect upon all the work and reflection you've done as you've worked through this journal. Growth takes time and a commitment to developing new habits, but small shifts can put you on the path toward lasting change. Recognize and give yourself praise for all you have accomplished thus far. Now make a list of things you want to continue working on in the future. What measures can you take to keep revisiting and building upon your goals?

1. Set a timer for five minutes. Close your eyes and take a few deep breaths.
2. Imagine yourself in a calm space, real or imaginary.
3. Imagine a wise being approaches you—somebody safe and nurturing. It can be any type of being—a person, animal, spirit, or maybe just a presence. Just know this being is there to comfort and support you.
4. Spend time listening to any messages, receiving any guidance, and accepting any gifts this being has to offer.
5. When time is up, say goodbye to this wise being and come back to the present moment. Recognize that this being is your own intuition, there for you anytime you need it.

*"You have to grow from the inside out.
None can teach you, none can make you spiritual.
There is no other teacher but your own soul."*

—SWAMI VIVEKANANDA

A FINAL WORD ON SELF-CARE AND A FULFILLING FUTURE

Congratulations on making it through the seven core components of self-care! It takes a lot of hard work and an openness to being vulnerable to self-reflect and become more introspective. If you dove into the prompts, used the journaling spaces to unpack various questions as they relate to your own journey, and gave the practices a shot, you have a lot to be proud of.

I hope you gained valuable insight into some ways you can care for yourself in order to live a more fulfilling and happy life. Self-care is an ongoing process and something to keep working at throughout your life. Taking just a few minutes each day to prioritize self-care can help keep you strong and grounded amid all of life's ups and downs.

I encourage you to revisit this journal often to reflect on your self-observations, refresh your memory on tools and practices that can help you stay balanced, and celebrate your progress. You can even complete the prompts again, and make note of your progress each time. Continue to use the affirmations, working them into your daily self-talk—especially the ones that feel most challenging for you. You can "fake it till you make it." Indeed, by repeating these words, you literally rewire your brain.

If you would like more support in diving deeper into these concepts as they relate to your own journey, I encourage you to seek the help of a qualified mental health professional. Two resources for finding support include PsychologyToday.com and GoodTherapy.org. I also invite you to check out the resources page on my website, www.MeganMaccutcheon.com/resources, where you can find workshops and free resources that expand upon many of the topics we've explored.

In closing, I wish you joy and contentment on your ongoing self-care journey. I hope you'll treasure all the work you've put into this journal and reflect upon it often as you continue on your journey to becoming your best self. You are worth it!

REFERENCES

Brainy Quote. October 15, 2021. BrainyQuote.com.

Brown, Brené. *Daring Greatly: How the Courage to Be Vulnerable Transforms the Way We Live, Love, Parent, and Lead.* New York: Gotham Books, 2018.

Canfield, Jack, Stephanie Marston, and Mark Victor Hansen. *Life Lessons for Women: 7 Essential Ingredients for a Balanced Life.* New York: Chicken Soup for the Soul, 2013.

Clemmer, Jim. *The Leader's Digest: Timeless Principles for Team and Organization Success*. Toronto: ECW Press, 2003.

Frankl, Viktor Emil. *Man's Search for Meaning.* Boston: Beacon Press, 2006.

Goodreads. October 15, 2021. Goodreads.com/quotes.

Good Therapy. October 15, 2021. GoodTherapy.com.

Inspiring Quotes. October 15, 2021. InspiringQuotes.com.

Johnson, Tory. *Shift for Good: Simple Changes for Lasting Joy Inside and Out.* New York: Hachette Books, 2015.

Kondo, Marie. *The Life-Changing Magic of Tidying Up: The Japanese Art of Decluttering and Organizing.* Berkeley, CA: Ten Speed Press, 2014.

Neff, Kristin. *Self-Compassion: Stop Beating Yourself Up and Leave Insecurity Behind.* New York: HarperCollins, 2011.

Oprah.com. "Take Nate Home." Accessed November 6, 2021. Oprah.com/home/take-nate-berkus-home-with-you_1/all.

Oprah.com. "The 10 Best Things We Learned at *O's* Live Your Best Life Weekend." Accessed November 6, 2021. Oprah.com/health/inspirational-quotes-from-oprahs-live-your-best-life-weekend.

Psychology Today. October 15, 2021. PsychologyToday.com.

Rath, Tom, and Don Clifton. *How Full Is Your Bucket?* New York: Gallup Press, 2004.

Rath, Tom, and Mary Reckmeyer. *How Full Is Your Bucket? For Kids.* New York: Gallup Press, 2009.

ACKNOWLEDGMENTS

There are so many great self-care practices; more than I could ever include in one book. Practicing gratitude was one I found myself experiencing again and again while writing this book.

Thank you to my family: Spending quality time with you is my ultimate self-care. To my friends: All the laughter and memories give me incredible doses of self-care. I'm grateful for all the different spaces I found myself in while writing this book: The amazing trip we took to Casa de Campo, where I wrote much of part one (that was self-care on steroids!); the hammock out back where I proofread drafts; the rockers on my front porch where I typed away; my friend's mountain house where I reminded myself to practice what I preach—take deep breaths and enjoy all that nature has to offer.

Thank you to my editor, Chloe Moffett, and to Patty Consolazio. Also, thank you to my amazing assistant, Jessica, for all her help, especially when I have major mom brain.

And, thank *you*, reader, for embarking on this journey. Life is not always easy. Believing in our worth can be challenging. Making time for self-care takes effort. But I'm so grateful that you are trying. I hope you are inspired to move forward with a renewed sense of hope and a dedication to being your best.

ABOUT THE AUTHOR

Megan MacCutcheon is a licensed professional counselor and certified perinatal mental health practitioner in private practice in Northern Virginia. She specializes in working with moms who are experiencing stress or mood/anxiety disorders during pregnancy and following childbirth. She is also passionate about helping people achieve a better quality of life by healing from trauma, improving self-esteem, managing anxiety, and decreasing depression. She has published four previous books on the topic of building self-esteem and loves teaching about self-improvement topics. For more information and to access her workshops, please visit www.MeganMaccutcheon.com.

CPSIA information can be obtained
at www.ICGtesting.com
Printed in the USA
LVHW070115030322
712523LV00005B/61

9 781638 781196